FINDING BIRDS in the CHESAPEAKE MARSH

a child's first look

Zora Aiken

illustrated by David Aiken

Tidewater Publishers
Centreville, Maryland

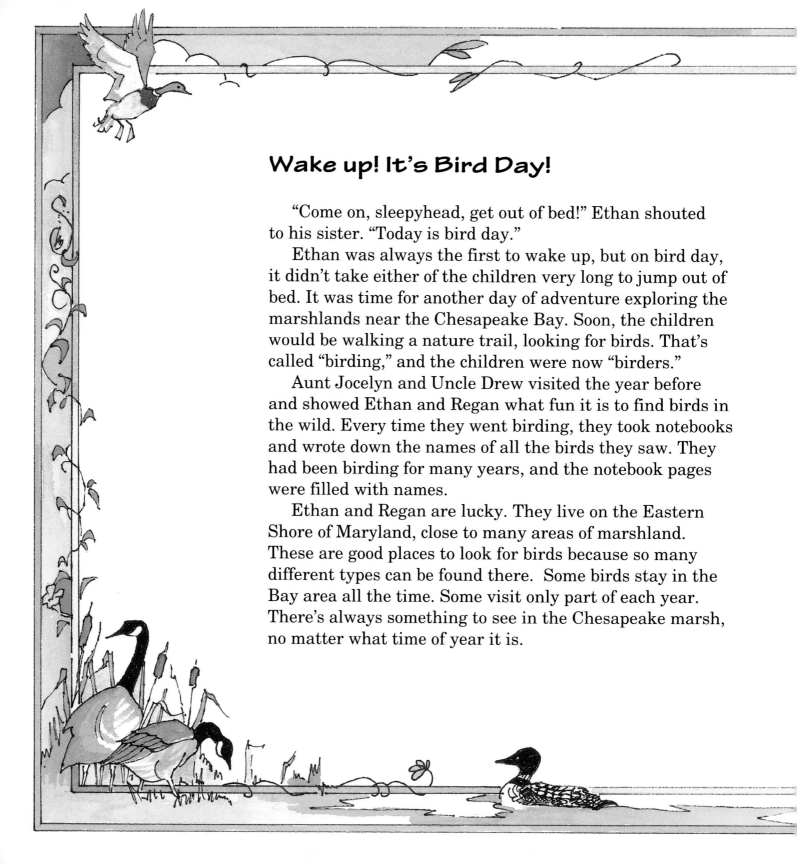

Wake up! It's Bird Day!

"Come on, sleepyhead, get out of bed!" Ethan shouted to his sister. "Today is bird day."

Ethan was always the first to wake up, but on bird day, it didn't take either of the children very long to jump out of bed. It was time for another day of adventure exploring the marshlands near the Chesapeake Bay. Soon, the children would be walking a nature trail, looking for birds. That's called "birding," and the children were now "birders."

Aunt Jocelyn and Uncle Drew visited the year before and showed Ethan and Regan what fun it is to find birds in the wild. Every time they went birding, they took notebooks and wrote down the names of all the birds they saw. They had been birding for many years, and the notebook pages were filled with names.

Ethan and Regan are lucky. They live on the Eastern Shore of Maryland, close to many areas of marshland. These are good places to look for birds because so many different types can be found there. Some birds stay in the Bay area all the time. Some visit only part of each year. There's always something to see in the Chesapeake marsh, no matter what time of year it is.

Ethan and Regan started their own bird lists the first time they went birding. They always carry their notebooks, and they take binoculars too, special eyeglasses that help them watch birds even when they are far away.

"We'll go to the wildlife refuge, Regan," said Ethan. "We're sure to find birds there."

They dressed quickly. Their mom drove to the refuge, a place where rangers take care of the land and keep it safe for the birds. It's a lovely wilderness area full of ponds and creeks and pine trees and marsh grass. The place is very peaceful, too—it's nice to be able to hear nature's sounds.

At the office of the refuge, the ranger gave each child a map and pictures of the birds they would try to find. Soon the children were hiking on a path near a winding creek.

"When we see a new bird, we'll add its name to our lists," said Ethan, "but from now on, let's write down more than just the bird's name. Every time we see a new bird, let's write down where it was and how we found it. We can even draw pictures. We'll make a whole book this way, so we can show all our friends why birding is so neat."

"Okay," agreed Regan. "Let's get going!"

Great Blue Heron

"Bet you can't get close to that bird," said Regan. "Watch what happens!"

The two had spotted a great blue heron wading in the shallow water. It was a big, tall, grayish blue bird with long, thin legs. When hunting for its dinner of fish, the great blue heron stands very quietly near the edge of a pond or creek, watching the water and waiting for a fish to swim near. If you try to sneak up for a closer look, the bird leaps into flight with a loud squawk. At a safe distance, the heron lands and once again stares into the water. But as many times as you try to get close, that's how many times it will squawk and fly away.

Great blue herons are seen all over the United States. Many spend the winter south of the Chesapeake area, but some stay all year.

The great blue heron "preens" its feathers (keeps them neat) by using a tiny "comb" that is part of its foot.

Another large heron visits the Bay too—it is almost the same size as the great blue, but it is all white. This is the great egret.

The large herons have some smaller cousins too: one is the little blue heron.

Snowy Egret

"I like snowy egrets," said Regan. "I even like the sound of the name!"

"Yes," said Ethan. "The name of the bird tells you what to look for."

Smaller than a great blue heron and pure white, the snowy egret is very pretty and dainty as it moves along the shoreline on thin black legs, looking for its supper. It may spring into action suddenly and start to run back and forth, perhaps to scare the fish. When the fish try to swim away, the egret will be able to see them better.

At times, the snowy egret ruffles its head feathers into a filmy crest and fluffs its chest feathers at the same time. People once caught these birds just to use their feathers in hats. The law doesn't allow that now—feathers belong on birds, not on hats.

Some people think a cattle egret is a snowy egret. The cattle egret is all white too, but it is smaller and has a shorter neck. It is usually found in fields rather than at shorelines; it eats insects stirred up by animals walking in the pasture. The cattle egret's legs are yellow. The snowy egret has black legs and yellow feet—it's called "the bird with the golden slippers."

Green Heron

"What's the little green bird hiding under that branch?" asked Regan.

"That one's easy," said Ethan. "It's a green heron. People used to call this bird the green-backed heron, and I think that's a better name because it gives you a good idea of what you'll see."

This small heron is about the size of a crow. It does not spend much time in open pond areas, where it might be seen more easily. Instead, it will usually be found along the shore of a river or creek.

A good way to spot a green heron is to look for it while drifting along the creek in a canoe. Because a canoe moves so quietly, you can get quite close to the heron without scaring it away. The bird is often seen clinging to a low tree branch that hangs out over the water, waiting for small fish to swim into view.

The green heron's face and neck are reddish brown, its back muddy green, and its legs bright yellow. It would be hard to mistake this small heron for any other bird.

Red-Winged Blackbird and Marsh Wren

"I didn't think a red-winged blackbird would be found in the same place as the wading birds," said Ethan.

"It is funny," said Regan. "But they're at home in the marsh. Many live here all year."

The red-winged blackbird brings a spot of color to a marshland that is mostly green in the summer and wheat-color in the fall. This bird is always part of the scene, perched on a cattail, swinging with the breeze and singing a song. The male bird is all black except for the small red patch and thin yellow band on his wings. The female is a streaked dark brown.

Blackbirds share the marsh with other perching birds, like the marsh wren. Because of their size and color, these tiny birds are not very easy to find. The color of their feathers—a mix of brown and white—fades into the background of cattails and reeds.

A wren's nest looks like a hollow ball. The male bird may build many nests, to fool any animals or larger birds who might try to steal the eggs. Sometimes, when the birds move out of the nest, mice move in.

Laughing Gull

"You don't need a picture to find a laughing gull," said Regan.

"That's right," answered Ethan. "Just listen and you won't have to look. People always think of the seashore when they hear gulls, because many kinds of gulls live along the shore."

"They seem to enjoy playing games," said Regan, as she watched a group of gulls take turns chasing each other off the big round posts holding the dock. "I call this game 'king of the post,' but no gull is king for very long."

Gulls fly in noisy flocks. They often follow fishing boats out on the water. Children chase gulls on the beach just to watch them fly and land.

The laughing gull is smaller than other types of gulls. In the summer, its head is black, so even if there are no other gulls nearby to check the size, you can be sure which one you have found. The gull's beak turns down at the end, giving the bird a stern look that does not match its laughing call.

In the winter, the birds travel as far south as South America. In its winter plumage, the laughing gull's head is mostly white.

Osprey

"We were lucky to find Captain Wayne today," Ethan said. "It's fun to ride on a real workboat, like this 'skipjack.' The captain uses the boat to gather oysters every fall, but in the summer, he takes people out to see the sights on the Bay."

Along the river channel, the boat passed a number of markers—posts and platforms with numbers and lights that tell boat captains which way to steer the boat. Some ospreys like to build their nests on these platforms, and in the spring, a nest may be home to two or three osprey babies too. The adult birds don't like boats to come too close. They fly about and make a noisy racket, trying to chase the boats away.

Ospreys eat fish, so they are also called fish hawks. To catch a fish, an osprey circles high above the water, then dives into the water feet first and comes up holding a fish with the talons on its feet. The fish's head is always pointed forward. This makes it easier for the bird to fly.

Ospreys can be found in the Bay from spring to fall. They leave in September or October and spend winter farther south.

Bald Eagle

"Look at the size of that bird!" shouted Ethan. "It must be a bald eagle. See? It has a white head."

Often, a bald eagle is seen sitting in a tall, dead tree. Here, the bird has a good view of the activity below, and people have a good view of the bird, since no leaves can get in the way.

The nest of a bald eagle is usually in a very high place, sometimes on a cliff overlooking water. In a wooded area, the nest may be in a tall pine tree.

The bald eagle is big, strong, and beautiful—some people say majestic. That's why it was chosen to be the national bird of the United States. The adult bird is dark brown with a white head and tail. It takes four years for a baby eaglet to grow up and show these white markings.

Two other birds might be mistaken for eagles: ospreys and turkey vultures are similar in size, but each bird flies in a different way. The eagle holds its wings straight out, the osprey's wings point up in the middle, and a turkey vulture's wings curve up at the ends.

BALD EAGLE   OSPREY   TURKEY VULTURE

Mallard

"Do mallards stay in the Chesapeake all year?" asked Regan. "We see them with their babies in the spring, and they're here in the fall too."

"A long time ago, all the mallards migrated," said Ethan, "just like the geese and tundra swans. Today, many mallards still migrate, but some live here all year."

The male mallard (the drake) has bright, almost shiny green feathers on his head and a narrow stripe of blue on his wings. The female (the hen) is not as pretty as the drake. She is spotty brown all over, which makes her look very much like another kind of duck, the "black duck," although the mallard hen is a lighter color.

Mallards are "dabbling" ducks. That means they eat underwater plants, and to do so, they must tip their bodies up so their heads can go under the surface of the water. It's fun to watch a group of ducks as they tip up, sit down, then tip up again, over and over.

You can see many mallard families in the spring. Ducklings can walk and swim just a few hours after they hatch. The fuzzy babies follow the mother everywhere. They grow very quickly.

Canvasback and Redhead

"Is that a canvasback?" asked Regan.

"I'm not sure," said Ethan. "It has a rust-colored head and a gray back, but so does a redhead. We'll have to ask the ranger how to tell them apart."

Canvasbacks will most likely be found in the fall and winter in a larger, open bay. (People call canvasbacks "cans.") The redheads may stay in a more protected place, like the mouth of a river. Both are diving ducks—they dive under the water and swim to their food. Mostly, they eat water plants. When they want to fly, they appear to run along the water's surface to get started.

When you see the canvasback from the side, its head looks more flat on top than the redhead's. The canvasback's neck is longer, its back is lighter gray, and its bill is longer, darker, and more pointed. But it is still hard to tell which is which when you don't see them at the same time.

Like the other waterfowl that visit the Bay, both ducks migrate every year in the spring and fall. They breed mainly in the prairie lands of the United States and Canada.

Tundra Swan

"When you see swans far away, you can't tell how big they are, but up close, wow!" said Regan.

"Yes," agreed her brother, "they're very big and they're not friendly, so be careful if you ever do get close."

In mid-November, the beautiful white tundra swans fly from Canada's Arctic coast and Alaska's North Slope, arriving in the Chesapeake in great flocks. A very graceful bird, the tundra swan swims with its neck straight up and its head straight out. Sometimes, its tail points straight up, too. Swans also "tip up" to eat underwater plants.

The tundra swan has a black bill and a small spot of yellow at the place where the bill touches the bird's face.

Another kind of swan, the mute swan, also lives in the Bay area now. In the spring, it is common to see families of mute swans—mom, dad, and two or three young "cygnets"—all swimming in a line along the bank of a creek.

Because mute swans are not "native" to the Bay, people call them "invasive."

The mute swan has a bright orange bill with a large black knob on it. When swimming, it curves its neck into the shape of an "S."

Canada Goose

"It's exciting to see a flock of Canada geese fly in to a creek," said Ethan. "First you hear the loud 'honk' of their call, then the sound of their wings. The sky is filled with birds, flying in a single row or lined up in a 'V.'"

"I like the way they land in the water," said Regan, "with their feet out front so the splash stops them. Then they quickly tuck in their wings and wiggle their tails."

When geese mate, the pair stays together as long as both are healthy. Some geese live in the Chesapeake all year, but most nest in Canada, where each pair has two or three "goslings." In the fall, huge flocks of geese fly south to spend winter in the Bay area. In spring, they head north again.

People do not know how the geese find their way back and forth, or how they know when it's time to fly. It is one of nature's mysteries.

Snow geese also fly in from Canada. Smaller than Canada geese, snow geese are almost pure white, with just a touch of black at the end of their wings.

Geese and other waterfowl eat the seeds and roots of a marsh plant or "sedge" called Olney three-square.

Common Loon

"Loons live in the water almost their whole lives," said Ethan.

"They must get tired of swimming all the time," said Regan.

"No, they can swim more easily than they can walk. Look far out into the water and see if you can spot one. A loon is bigger than a duck, but it sits farther down in the water so you don't see as much of its back."

In the summer, most loons live farther north, but a few stay near the Chesapeake. Their feathers show a beautiful black-and-white pattern. In the fall, when more loons are in the Bay, they have their winter feathers, which are dark brownish gray.

The loon's eyes are red; this may help them see better underwater. Males and females look exactly alike. The loon's call is almost musical, but it's not a song that people can sing— it's a very special sound.

Like other migrating birds, loons fly to a different place to raise their young. They build their nests along the shore of an island in Canada or the upper Midwest. Baby loons are lucky—when they are very little, they often ride on their mother's back.

By the end of the day, the children had added many names and pictures to their notebooks.

"What's next?" asked Regan.

"More trips, more places, more birds," answered Ethan. "The marsh birds are only the start of our birding fun."